Footprints In Time

A. DEE HUXLEY

Published in 2017 by FeedARead Publishing

First Edition

Cover design by A. Dee Huxley and zodshopdesign.co.uk
Logo design by A. Dee Huxley
All design copyrights © 2017 A. Dee Huxley

British Library C.I.P.

A CIP catalogue record for this title is
available from the British Library.

for...

*All those individuals, both human and furry ones,
who have shared my life's journey. Thank you for
each cherished memory. I have truly been grateful to
every love-inspired moment.*

*Those, who I never had the privilege to meet in time
or space, who shared their wisdom leaving breadcrumbs
for us all to follow. Those global strands of ancient
wisdom remain the watermarks of all our lives.*

*Our lovely, magnificent and beautifully glorious planetary
home, Mother Earth ; Gaia. Without you, none of this
would have been dreamed of or made possible.*

*with love,
Dee*

Contents

Falling In Love

Love's Journey

In flowers of youth
I garland my love,
in bright radiant sunshine
from heavens above,
in pastures of green
I trip endlessly through,
on a wondrous journey
to wonderful you.

In life everlasting
I caress you my dear,
through dawns never ending
I'll transcend to here,
following loyally,
with merest of light,
your body, your shadow,
far into the night.

I know not where you'll lead me,
but of this I am sure,
that whatever encountered
our love will endure,
for you see I do love you,
for always I've known,
that without your love
I am truly alone.

Here

Here, as I hold you in my arms,
I know that love is here,
surrounding us and calm,
taking away my fear.

Here, as I drift into the night,
I look upon your face,
knowing that my soul
was touched by your embrace.

All of my life
I've dreamed of meeting love,
and now I hold it close,
a breath,
a heartbeat away.

Here, as I think about my life,
protected from all harm,
I know a peace within,
your love has brought such calm.

Here, as I reach to touch your face,
I hear your heart call,
you smile, the world is mine,
I know that love is all.

Love's Dream

I lie awake
within my bed,
and ponder on the words
you've said.

You spoke of love,
of you with me,
of wondrous dreams
we both shall see.

I stretch my hand
and touch your face,
and remember fondly
your loving embrace.

We are united,
body and mind,
as others have felt,
in their own space and time.

I turn and smile
at my gentle lover,
who could have the world,
but needs no other.

Dream on,
till this night is past,
our daydreams together tomorrow
begin, and all of them will last.

Separating

Echoes of my love
fill my brain,
thoughts of them
in sad refrain.
I see a world
within their eyes,
a gift of love
that is my prize.

A hurt though,
hangs suspended there,
a feeling of pain
that fills the air.
Night falls so quickly
when time is needed,
to say things that are felt
but still unheeded.

A world that surpasses
all is what I see,
distant visions
of you with me.

Shadows ever fleeting,
I cannot hold.
Memories half forgotten,
half untold,
transcend us
to an empty place,
that holds not love
upon its face.

Please take us back
where we belong,
and sing with me
a sweeter song,
of love, of life,
of you with me,
of wondrous dreams
that we will see.

I need your love.
I know for all time,
that I am yours.
Will you be mine ?

When Love Dies

In your face, so much pain
my heart wants to cry,
for it reflects a love
that's been condemned to die.

Once it was perfect,
but once has now gone.
Now a loving couple
is one against one.

How can we sit here,
afraid to say,
caring words to take
the hurt away ?

What do we fear ?
Are we really so vain,
to kill our love,
then not even explain.

To hold a noose above
our heart,
tighten the rope,
then just turn and part.

Time has tricked us
into this place,
where love no longer
shows its face.

Where hearts no longer flutter,
nor pulses pound,
where all affection is
stifled from sound.

We sit here smiling
at a faceless stranger,
unaware, uncaring
of the impending danger.

I see your face etched
with such fear,
accepting our fate,
not knowing I'm near.

Eyes that would sparkle,
now lifeless and dull,
hatred's vessel
now bitterly full.

We have reached the parting,
each counting our cost.
Pain without pity.
Love without loss.

Heart And Soul

I loved you.
You feared me,
feared what I would take
from your soul.
You pushed me away,
but not too far
so you were cold.

We were each like
sparring animals,
circling to determine
the other's weakness.
At last I understand ;
not your frailty,
but my strength.

And know what I would have
taken from your soul,
if you had let me.
Loneliness ; grief ; separation ;
apathy ; doubt.

And what I would have
given to your soul,
if you had let me.
Unity joy harmony
passion certainty.

I could tell you that
I understand your fear.

I could promise
that I will wait
a lifetime for you.

But they would both be lies.

And so I leave you,
with no reason to fear.

I Never Needed You More

I never needed you
more than I do now.
Never felt the passion
as I now feel it flow.

Nor did I perceive
the blueness of your eyes,
holding all those gifts of love.
Was I ever worthy of the prize ?

The blondeness of your hair
never before meant much to me,
now it all invades my vision,
it's all that I can see.

Nor did I speak of my love
and tell you true,
that I longed to know the depths,
and heights, of you.

Words that come easily
with the passage of space and time
seemed hesitant back then,
out of step ; out of rhyme.

The joy within your laughter
that made the world fade away,
never pierced my heart before,
but it's broken it today.

Be Still My
Breaking Heart

The world
keeps turning
as your memory fades.
My heart has now stopped
yearning, for the return
of bygone days.

The stars still
shine as brightly,
as they have before.
A symbol of a greater light,
that opens
the knocked-upon door.

And as your face
dims within my eyes,
I glimpse a better, happier life,
the promise of a love that never dies,
even though you so skilfully
wielded the knife.

So goodbye my love.
To what,
I cannot say.
For now
I hold no hope for you,
tomorrow or today.

Remember Me

In the future,
if your thoughts ever turn to me ;
allow me some dignity
in the vision that you see.

Smile at all the actions,
some silly, some vain,
a mixed-up performer
reading lines unexplained.

Ponder on the past, I hope,
with a little tenderness ;
remember all our good times,
allow yourself its best.

And take no bitterness
or dispassion from our stage,
where the feelings were
from another place and age.

And when nights are drawing in,
allow your mind to drift
to the greater destination
we were never meant to meet.

Through the glorious dawns
that each must view alone,
remember that sometime, somewhere,
each finds their own way home.

And if you cry,
let the tears be tears of joy,
for even though we tried so hard,
our love is not destroyed.

Hold your life within your hand
caress it like a dream,
realise all your visions
even those as yet unseen.

The past is dead and gone now,
and that's the way it should be.
But remember it with laughter,
and compassion, if you ever think of me.

The Invitation

Please,
come dance with me.
Let us create
a rhythm and tempo
of our own.

Let us permit our souls
to touch with freed abandon,
and respond
to the candescence
of our love.

Allow our lives
to become a testament,
to the cosmic dance ;
of stars, universes, of every atom.
Vibrant and strong,
separate yet co-joined.

Let everyone
who witnesses
our dance sing the praises
of their Creator,
and know that the dance goes on.

Let them breathe
deeply and sigh,
and surrender to the pulse
of their soul, and join
the glorious dance, of life.

My Promise

I'd share the gift of life with you,
if it were mine to give.
I'd even conquer death for you,
so for ever you may live.

No vision that belonged to me,
would be hidden from your sight.
All the gifts that I possess,
would belong to you by right.

And finally, when you know it all,
no longer needing me.
Then from your vision I will fall,
then truly I'd be free.

Eternal Love

We lived
a dream of life,
played our drama
on the edge of a knife.

Time and time
we tricked our fate,
always making
the reaper wait.

We glimpsed
the haunted souls of them,
who felt afraid
to love again.

Climbing to the glorious
heights within,
where all exists,
where there is no sin.

Never
was there a hint of doubt
within our souls,
we cast it out.

No remorse
for our losses was ever seen,
upon our love's
wondrous dream.

We sang the songs
that others could not hear,
lived our thoughts of beauty
with no hint of fear.

And now at last,
we behold the verse,
written at the heart
of the universe.

Our Fracturing World

Here And Now

We ponder
on life up in the skies,
and listen
to those who say they are wise.

Never a thought
of Here and Now
enters our minds
and is allowed to grow.

Always considering
the future, the past,
not enjoying Now,
until its time has elapsed.

The Time Has Come

A path lies before me,
its destination is my home.
As I stand at its beginning,
I wonder why I roamed.

The yearning that lies inside me,
to once again behold,
visions held in Dreamtime,
where miracles unfold.

My heart, my very soul,
is crying out for the peace,
that's held within my grasp,
now the strife within has ceased.

But as I look around me,
I witness hate and fear,
a corruption so strong,
it makes the truth unclear.

I see a world that's dying,
with it all my dreams die too,
hoping for a chance
to help the Earth renew.

It is the very Soul,
we are tearing from Her heart,
certain of our right,
to condemn nature from the start.

The Earth was not created
to be the dustbin for our race.
Other creatures were not born
to have horror etched upon their face.

The time is growing short now,
the time has come to stand,
for hope, that springs eternal,
give nature a helping hand.

Just close your eyes,
and feel the power of our Earth.
Don't sound Her death knell,
witness Her re-birth.

The Spirit Of Loving

Loving soars us
upon eagle's wings.
Lifting us onward
to greater things.

Passions arise
in tumultuous sound.
Tearing all those shackles
that held us aground.

Oh sing of the wondrous
life that we live !
Cry for the heart-less
unable to give.

Fight for the needy
battle-torn and scared.
Conquer the mighty
who couldn't have cared.

Grieve for the young
who still feel unafraid.
Die for the old
for the world they have made.

Ancient Is Modern

The universe is within me,
it lies within us all.
United in Dreamtime
we were led by nature's call.

But something long ago
made it all go awry,
taking from our souls divinity,
making truth die.

We may think we are winning,
that nature has lost.
But it's a hollow victory,
in the terms of the cost.

For the Earth is playing by
Her own eternal rules.
We may be technologically intelligent,
but in life's game, we are mere fools.

The end is so close now.
Reach out, touch the truth.
Ancient is modern.
Age has its youth.

Managing Change

We put on labels
of good and bad ;
the things we want,
the things we've had.

The Earth becomes a mere object
to accept, or to deny.
Life simply an amusement,
where we laugh and sometimes cry.

All a little boring. A little strange.
A little wrong.
All a little threatening,
if we feel we don't belong.

We move from right to left,
And then again from left to right,
rethinking our daily decisions
over and over through the night.

Then somehow, in the sunset
of our life, we wonder why,
that with all this change around us,
we have never learnt to die.

That with all the beauty
that the universe can give,
we had only learnt to cope.
And have never learnt to live.

Vindictive Leisure

She stands
before a pointed gun,
her life will end,
for its owner's fun.
Her days
no longer filled with pleasure,
a victim
of vindictive leisure.

Her face
no longer will be seen,
upon this Earth
that is so green.
Her eyes
will never again respond to light,
nor sense
the wonders of the night.

The hunter
has slain you,
who once roamed free.
But with you,
died
a part of me.

Yes They Say It Was

The year is 1914,
I'm a worker for the state.
I'm walking home alone,
the time is half past eight.

Someone has started a war
and I've got to go and fight,
because this is the war
to end all wars.

The year is 1918.
I've returned from fighting
in the war to end all wars.

But how can war end war,
how can wrong right wrong,
how can people say
that people will not fight ?

Yes, they say it was the war,
yes, they say it was the war,
yes, they say it was the war
to end all wars.

The year is 1939,
I'm a veteran of the state ;
they've started another war
but this time I can't fight.

And whether in British
or in German
they will say,
"this is the war
to end all wars".

And in a few years time
when I'm no longer here,
they'll start another war
and if anyone can still hear,
I wonder who will dare
say ; "this was
the war to end all wars".

Why can't we ever learn,
that war cannot end war,
that war cannot breed love.

Yes, they'll say
that war ends war,
yes, they'll say
that wrong rights wrong,
yes, they'll say
that people will not fight.

Ah yes, I well
recall the year of 1918,
when I came home filled
with so much hope,
after fighting in the war
to end all wars.

Shattered Peace

The world feels no hint of regret
for the tortures witnessed
in peaceful Tibet,
for in the West
there is nothing finer
than selling goods
to the virgin China.

They focus on trade and forget the fear,
shown in the eyes of Tibetan
children, living so near
the sun. In the cool clean air
in a land that once was,
all that others dreamed of,
in their search for God.

The people whose ways
are peaceful and just,
now witness their culture
trampled in the dust.

The Tibet of old is fading fast,
a culture of a millennium
surely can't last
this onslaught, by aliens
from a foreign land,
who bring hate and violence
the Tibetans simply can't understand.

The pearls of wisdom are now hidden deep,
given to those who
have the power to keep
their unique truth and justice,
held above all earthly things,
the Chinese can't cope
with the love that this brings.

This land, this Tibet,
holds no place for you,
and all in the U.N.
know that to be true.
But the one thing you lack Tibet,
the land of milk and honey,
is the power of influence,
which goes under the name ...

Money.

The Orang-utan's Meaning

You live in the forest
of Borneo,
becoming more isolated
from your world of old.

Wondering when the
men will return,
to remove your home ;
or your life.

Sitting majestically at the
roof of the forest,
you are a silent witness
to all we wish to hide
from ourselves
and others.

Our incessant search
for more,
but more of what ?
More money.
More things.
Less trees,
less breath.

I can live without that table,
without that wardrobe,
you cannot live
without a Home.

In 2025 will my children
recognise the true cost of that table.
Will they condemn me
with unspoken words ?

Will they mourn the loss they feel,
what we all should feel ?
For the sake of a dining table and chairs,
a species was lost.

Should that be engraved
into tree trunks,
or into our hearts
and souls ?

Gaia Dreaming

Our Gentle Reminder

Through the glorious dawn-stroked sky
I hear the Earth's quiet voice ...

"Will you leave me to die
while you still have the choice.
What is evident to see
is you can't live without me.
What is equally true
is I can live without you."

On The Other Side

On the other side,
there lies a world
that through our fears we hide.

Where pebbles on the shore
are caressed by waves of aqua green,
and trees silhouetted
by a silvery moonbeam.

Where strands of gold
entwine the hearts of each with all,
and none are deaf
to another's needing call.

Tigers and elephants
roam free upon the plains so green,
unafraid of the guns
that they have never seen.

And humankind stands
erect and tall,
not over-sized,
or small.

Where each embraces the web of life
and respects each different strand,
their days are filled with peace
and grace of hand.

Is this world really
on the other side.
Or is it here,
and in our fears we hide ?

New Beginnings

We came
out of the primal soup
into a world devoid of life,
scratching the surface
of the Earth
to acknowledge
our existence.

Moving onward
away from the shoreline
waves of pulsating energy
driving our bodies,
limbs stretching cut by
jagged rocks as our skin
is confronted by alien land.

Lungs tasting dry air
ripping passed our throat,
we cry, hearing
our voices for the first time.

We scream
for the realm of peace
we have left,
tormented by memories
of harmonious existence,
where bodies were suspended
in tranquil movement.

We yearn
to return to the ocean
but our bodies crawl away ;
new life has come to the Earth
we can no longer
return to the sea
that is our curse.

Universal Song

Sometime, when you
have a moment free,
close your eyes
and you will see
a song that has been sung
since the universe began,
of our union with God's
eternal plan.

It echoes
all around,
singing with
abundant sound ;
the beat pulsates
within your heart,
making the cares
of this world depart.

The birds, the trees,
the animals, all hear
this song that is muted
to us by our fear.

The tune that says,
"we are home,
naught is lost,
all has just begun."

Avalon Dreams

I dream of Avalon
of days gone past,
the star-filled night
the beating drum,
the calling of tides
the wisdom of Age,
all is before us
nothing has begun.

I dream of Morgaine
the Queen of All,
the Sorceress of wisdom
running with the stag,
flying with the hawk
calling back the mists
to see the other-world.

And yet.

In the midst
of noise and confusion
we can still hear the silence,
and in that silence
if we have courage
and belief in ourselves,
we can part the mists
and perceive the truth.

Winter Tales

Winter draws in,
the Earth's
as cold as ice.
Unyielding,
asleep,
awaiting the one
who will be sacrificed.

Slowly each day,
the energy fades away,
gently dying,
peacefully leaving,
to awaken
upon another day.

The circle is
nearly complete,
on another year.
Another life.

Birth – spring.
Action – summer.
Re-collection – autumn.
And winter's death.

And so it goes,
from one year
to another.
Always moving,
nothing static.

Going
nowhere.
Going
somewhere.
Life goes.

But where it goes
no-one knows.
Or those that know,
do not tell.
Such is
the mystery.

The Unicorn's Gift

Silhouetted by the moon
the unicorn stands aloft
dancing with the rhythm
of the skies.

A symbol of a truth
we have long forgot
although we still search
for the prize.

His hooves pound
upon the Earth
echoing through the aeons
of time.

Demanding The Goddess'
re-birth
into a world with no reason
or rhyme.

His horn glints
with the moon-rays
his eyes sparkle
in the dead of night.

A symbol of truth
a reminder of better days
the incessant struggle
of eternal justice over might.

He stands upon
the mountain high
above humankind, he knows
he can touch the sky.

Knowing

Seize the day.
With all your hope and vision
make it yours in every way.

Seize the hour.
With strength and wisdom
fill it with so much power.

Seize the moment.
With grace and peace
allow that moment an eternity,
never let it cease.

Seize the second.
With pride and humility
and in that second,
you will be truly free.

Eloquent Seasons

In springtime
it was born ;

summer's light
made it bloom,

autumn leaves
saw its flaws,

in winter's darkness
it was finally entombed.

The Forgotten Lake

The silver moon
is shimmering,
on the shores
of a forgotten lake.
For the Lady no longer calls
the mists away,
to make this
scene awake.

And unicorns no longer
quench their thirst,
as they did
in ages old.
The songs of the bards,
and the tales of heroes,
along the shoreline
go untold.

For disharmony
has come between us,
between this lake
and I.
For I live in a world
where there are no mysteries,
or no beliefs
that make us fly.

Will the Lady ever return
to the shoreline of Her lake.
Will the unicorn be quenched
by the waters fresh and clear ?

How silly !
How absolutely human, to believe,
that because I cannot see the scene
it is no longer here.

For the Lady in all Her glory
stands beside the waterfall,
which feeds
and nurtures the lake,
as the lake, in turn,
nurtures all.

The unicorn still plays
with the lion and the lamb,
myths are still told
and legends animate the land.

How shallow do our lives appear,
when compared with such as these,
for something deep within us all
reminds us, we are them.

If only we could look within,
to the depths of ourselves
and awake ;

we may see the moon again,
reflected in the lake.

Earth Chant

Let us
go to the water
and behold a vision there,
of a truth beyond all glory
and knowledge beyond fear.
Let us flow
with the power
that the stream alone can give,
and let's know that in its waters
we are purified by love.

Let us
go to the mountains
where the air is fresh and pure,
let us sing to all nations
of the unity of all.
Let the life-blood
that's within us
beat the pulse of harmony,
and let's know that through each other
we are finally set free.

Let us
go to the valley
where there's minerals and stone,
let us know that our hearts must blend
with those as yet unknown.
Let us scream
to the valley
and hear Her soft reply,
keep faith with this Earth of ours
and then She will not die.

Let us
go to the animals
before we kill them all,
let us know that their fear of man
should not be there at all.
Let us roar
with the passion of
the jungle in the night,
and let's know that with them at our side
this is a winning fight.

Let us
go to the people
and awake them from their dream,
let us show them the miracles
of this Earth that is so green.
Let us weep
with an anger
for the death of what is right,
but let's know that God's spirit shines
through the darkest night.

About Spirit

Awakening

Glimpse the truth
within your soul.

Your life's dream
has been
slumbering
for too long.

It will awaken.

Not to a lover's kiss.

But to the sound
of your own heart.

Searching For ...
My Higher Self

Where are you now ?

Gone into the night,
leaving me alone
to conquer my fears.
To strive with
unfathomable questions,
and to yearn.

Yearn for what I've lost,
what we all
have lost,
by turning away
from our true self,
and dreaming
only of this world.

Push the veil away
a little, just a little,
what do you see,

can you find words
to emulate that vision.
Can you touch it, feel it.

Or is it so fragile a sight
that to utter a mere word
makes it vanish.
Does your heart not pound
with passion
and with fear.

I release the veil
and a sense of serenity
overwhelms me.

So far, yet so near,
only a heart-beat away,
a caress upon the air.

I have tonight borne witness
to the reality of
another world,
and where were you ?

Here.

And now I know
you'll never leave me.

What Can I Say

If I could write of how things are,
what words could express
that which I wished to convey.

What sounds could be uttered
from my mouth,
to be held upon the air
until your ears
caressed their meaning.

I only know that
I know nothing.
What words
convey no-thing.
What words
truly capture the majesty of life.

All I can say, is.
Life is – Here, and, Now.

Live it.
And it will live in you.

And through you,
all will behold
the wonder of it all.

Zen Thoughts

The bottle at last is broken,
in pieces it lies all around.
But not a word was spoken,
for it has no need of sound.

Taoist Dreams

You were always part of my soul,
a life lived many times,
an endless search for love,
through different form and age.

Mountains become valleys,
deserts spring to life,
stars explode in vibrant light,
then all noise becomes peace.

We are the two
halves of a whole,
the yin and yang
that becomes the Tao.

We exist
in the thoughts of those
who strive for love,
who seek it in tokens – bright
though hollow, yet
who desire the completion
of true, real love.

You and I
merge into One,
and leave
the dreams of man
to those who know
only duality.

Indestructible

Let me fly
on eagle wings
and leave
the world behind,
let me transcend
the wisdom
I could behold
when I was here on Earth.

Let my song
become the wind
that caresses your
well-remembered face,
and my soul
forever hold you
in an eternal loving embrace.

Let your memories
of me only bring you
laughter and joy,
and let your heart remember,
that the love we shared
death cannot destroy.

Come,
sit beside the water,
and let your grief
be washed away,
for I am there with you,
tomorrow and today.

The Ties Of Love

Love binds us all together,
not with ropes
or chains,
but by an all encompassing
expression of unity ;
flowing from one soul
to another.

A reminder that
the dance of life,
that resounds
throughout the universe,
enclosed in galaxies, stars,
planets and oceans,
pulsates within our veins,
within the very sinews
of our body.

Our hearts beat
to the universal rhythm,
a co-joining
of all humanity
in the eternal embrace
of love.

Each and every
soul participating
and renewing,
through the glorious
majesty of life,
the exquisite
vibrancy of joy,
an ultimate
revelation of love
transcending words ;
beyond touch.

Making Choices

We all know
that at some time
our beloved Mother Earth
will be filled with peace
and love.

So let us all,
individually and collectively,
choose that place and time –
Here and Now.

About The Author

Dee believes that we are increasingly being asked to live our lives embedded within 24/7 market-based societies. Many of our home and work environments have become bastions of information and distraction overload. Our five senses are incessantly bombarded by a stress producing human-made ecosystem ; one that drowns out an inner spiritual life or denies its very existence.

She also passionately believes that the ethos and values of the Celtic, Native American and Taoist traditions remain pertinently valid and increasingly more relevant in today's globalised but disparate societies.

These traditions enable us all to create a space of connection ; a 'time-out' from externally-focussed living, so we can harness our own intrinsic values and provide clarity of purpose to our daily actions.

As part of her own 'slow down' life change, Dee left a long and successful career in UK central government when she recognised that she could no longer be an agent of positive sustainable change.

Dee now lives in coastal Wales, with her partner and furry friends. She now focuses on writing, listening to nature's rhythms and continues her study of these ancient traditions.

Dee's books:

Footprints In Time   (2017)